Easter Day by Robert Browning

Robert Browning is one of the most significant Victorian Poets and, of course, English Poetry.

Much of his reputation is based upon his mastery of the dramatic monologue although his talents encompassed verse plays and even a well-regarded essay on Shelley during a long and prolific career.

He was born on May 7th, 1812 in Walmouth, London. Much of his education was home based and Browning was an eclectic and studious student, learning several languages and much else across a myriad of subjects, interests and passions.

Browning's early career began promisingly. The fragment from his intended long poem Pauline brought him to the attention of Dante Gabriel Rossetti, and was followed by Paracelsus, which was praised by both William Wordsworth and Charles Dickens. In 1840 the difficult Sordello, which was seen as willfully obscure, brought his career almost to a standstill.

Despite these artistic and professional difficulties his personal life was about to become immensely fulfilling. He began a relationship with, and then married, the older and better known Elizabeth Barrett. This new foundation served to energise his writings, his life and his career.

During their time in Italy they both wrote much of their best work. With her untimely death in 1861 he returned to London and thereafter began several further major projects.

The collection Dramatis Personae (1864) and the book-length epic poem The Ring and the Book (1868-69) were published and well received; his reputation as a venerated English poet now assured.

Robert Browning died in Venice on December 12th, 1889.

Index of Contents

EASTER-DAY

I

How very hard it is to be
A Christian! Hard for you and me,
—Not the mere task of making real
That duty up to its ideal,
Effecting thus, complete and whole,
A purpose of the human soul—

For that is always hard to do;
But hard, I mean, for me and you
To realize it, more or less,
With even the moderate success
Which commonly repays our strife
To carry out the aims of life.
"This aim is greater," you will say,
"And so more arduous every way."
—But the importance of their fruits
Still proves to man, in all pursuits,
Proportional encouragement.
"Then, what if it be God's intent
That labor to this one result
Should seem unduly difficult?"
Ah, that 's a question in the dark—
And the sole thing that I remark
Upon the difficulty, this:
We do not see it where it is,
At the beginning of the race:
As we proceed, it shifts its place,
And where we looked for crowns to fall,
We find the tug 's to come,—that 's all.

II

At first you say, "The whole, or chief
Of difficulties, is belief.
Could I believe once thoroughly,
The rest were simple. What? Am I
An idiot, do you think,—a beast?
Prove to me, only that the least
Command of God is God's indeed,
And what injunction shall I need
To pay obedience? Death so nigh,
When time must end, eternity
Begin,—and cannot I compute,
Weigh loss and gain together, suit
My actions to the balance drawn,
And give my body to be sawn
Asunder, hacked in pieces, tied
To horses, stoned, burned, crucified,
Like any martyr of the list?
How gladly!—if I make acquist,
Through the brief minute's fierce annoy,
Of God's eternity of joy."

III

—And certainly you name the point
Whereon all turns: for could you joint
This flexile finite life once tight
Into the fixed and infinite,
You, safe inside, would spurn what 's out,
With carelessness enough, no doubt—
Would spurn mere life: but when time brings
To their next stage your reasonings,
Your eyes, late wide, begin to wink
Nor see the path so well, I think.

IV

You say, "Faith may be, one agrees,
A touchstone for God's purposes,
Even as ourselves conceive of them.
Could he acquit us or condemn
For holding what no hand can loose,
Rejecting when we can't but choose?
As well award the victor's wreath
To whosoever should take breath
Duly each minute while he lived—
Grant heaven, because a man contrived
To see its sunlight every day
He walked forth on the public way.
You must mix some uncertainty
With faith, if you would have faith be.
Why, what but faith, do we abhor
And idolize each other for—
Faith in our evil or our good,
Which is or is not understood
Aright by those we love or those
We hate, thence called our friends or foes?
Your mistress saw your spirit's grace,
When, turning from the ugly face,
I found belief in it too hard;
And she and I have our reward.
—Yet here a doubt peeps: well for us
Weak beings, to go using thus
A touchstone for our little ends,
Trying with faith the foes and friends;
—But God, bethink you! I would fain
Conceive of the Creator's reign
As based upon exacter laws
Than creatures build by with applause.

In all God's acts—(as Plato cries
He doth)—he should geometrize.
Whence, I desiderate" ...

V

I see!
You would grow as a natural tree,
Stand as a rock, soar up like fire.
The world 's so perfect and entire,
Quite above faith, so right and fit!
Go there, walk up and down in it!
No. The creation travails, groans—
Contrive your music from its moans,
Without or let or hindrance, friend!
That 's an old story, and its end
As old—you come back (be sincere)
With every question you put here
(Here where there once was, and is still,
We think, a living oracle,
Whose answers you stand carping at)
This time flung back unanswered flat,—
Beside, perhaps, as many more
As those that drove you out before,
Now added, where was little need.
Questions impossible, indeed,
To us who sat still, all and each
Persuaded that our earth had speech,
Of God's, writ down, no matter if
In cursive type or hieroglyph,—
Which one fact freed us from the yoke
Of guessing why He never spoke.
You come back in no better plight
Than when you left us,—am I right?

VI

So, the old process, I conclude,
Goes on, the reasoning 's pursued
Further. You own, "'T is well averred,
A scientific faith 's absurd,
—Frustrates the very end 't was meant
To serve. So, I would rest content
With a mere probability,
But, probable; the chance must lie
Clear on one side,—lie all in rough,

So long as there be just enough
To pin my faith to, though it hap
Only at points: from gap to gap
One hangs up a huge curtain so,
Grandly, nor seeks to have it go
Foldless and flat along the wall.
What care I if some interval
Of life less plainly may depend
On God? I 'd hang there to the end;
And thus I should not find it hard
To be a Christian and debarred
From trailing on the earth, till furled
Away by death.—Renounce the world!
Were that a mighty hardship? Plan
A pleasant life, and straight some man
Beside you, with, if he thought fit,
Abundant means to compass it,
Shall turn deliberate aside
To try and live as, if you tried
You clearly might, yet most despise.
One friend of mine wears out his eyes,
Slighting the stupid joys of sense,
In patient hope that, ten years hence,
'Somewhat completer,' he may say,
'My list of coleoptera!'
While just the other who most laughs
At him, above all epitaphs
Aspires to have his tomb describe
Himself as sole among the tribe
Of snuffbox-fanciers, who possessed
A Grignon with the Regent's crest.
So that, subduing, as you want,
Whatever stands predominant
Among my earthly appetites
For tastes and smells and sounds and sights,
I shall be doing that alone,
To gain a palm-branch and a throne,
Which fifty people undertake
To do, and gladly, for the sake
Of giving a Semitic guess,
Or playing pawns at blindfold chess."

VII

Good: and the next thing is,—look round
For evidence enough! 'T is found,
No doubt: as is your sort of mind,

So is your sort of search: you 'll find
What you desire, and that 's to be
A Christian. What says history?
How comforting a point it were
To find some mummy-scrap declare
There lived a Moses! Better still,
Prove Jonah's whale translatable
Into some quicksand of the seas,
Isle, cavern, rock, or what you please,
That faith might flap her wings and crow
From such an eminence! Or, no—
The human heart 's best; you prefer
Making that prove the minister
To truth; you probe its wants and needs,
And hopes and fears, then try what creeds
Meet these most aptly,—resolute
That faith plucks such substantial fruit
Wherever these two correspond,
She little needs to look beyond
And puzzle out who Orpheus was,
Or Dionysius Zagrias.
You 'll find sufficient, as I say,
To satisfy you either way;
You wanted to believe; your pains
Are crowned—you do: and what remains?
"Renounce the world!"—Ah, were it done
By merely cutting one by one
Your limbs off, with your wise head last,
How easy were it!—how soon past,
If once in the believing mood!
"Such is man's usual gratitude,
Such thanks to God do we return,
For not exacting that we spurn
A single gift of life, forego
One real gain,—only taste them so
With gravity and temperance,
That those mild virtues may enhance
Such pleasures, rather than abstract—
Last spice of which, will be the fact
Of love discerned in every gift;
While, when the scene of life shall shift,
And the gay heart be taught to ache,
As sorrows and privations take
The place of joy,—the thing that seems
Mere misery, under human schemes,
Becomes, regarded by the light
Of love, as very near or quite
As good a gift as joy before.

So plain is it that, all the more
A dispensation 's merciful,
More pettishly we try and cull
Briers, thistles, from our private plot,
To mar God's ground where thorns are not!"

VIII

Do you say this, or I?—Oh, you!
Then, what, my friend?—(thus I pursue
Our parley)—you indeed opine
That the Eternal and Divine
Did, eighteen centuries ago,
In very truth ... Enough! you know
The all-stupendous tale,—that Birth,
That Life, that Death! And all, the earth
Shuddered at,—all, the heavens grew black
Rather than see; all, nature's rack
And throe at dissolution's brink
Attested,—all took place, you think,
Only to give our joys a zest,
And prove our sorrows for the best?
We differ, then! Were I, still pale
And heartstruck at the dreadful tale,
Waiting to hear God's voice declare
What horror followed for my share,
As implicated in the deed,
Apart from other sins,—concede
That if He blacked out in a blot
My brief life's pleasantness, 't were not
So very disproportionate!
Or there might be another fate—
I certainly could understand
(If fancies were the thing in hand)
How God might save, at that day's price,
The impure in their impurities,
Give license formal and complete
To choose the fair and pick the sweet.
But there be certain words, broad, plain,
Uttered again and yet again,
Hard to mistake or overgloss—
Announcing this world's gain for loss,
And bidding us reject the same:
The whole world lieth (they proclaim)
In wickedness,—come out of it!
Turn a deaf ear, if you think fit,
But I who thrill through every nerve

At thought of what deaf ears deserve—
How do you counsel in the case?

IX

"I 'd take, by all means, in your place,
The safe side, since it so appears:
Deny myself, a few brief years,
The natural pleasure, leave the fruit
Or cut the plant up by the root.
Remember what a martyr said
On the rude tablet overhead!
'I was born sickly, poor and mean,
A slave: no misery could screen
The holders of the pearl of price
From Cæsar's envy; therefore twice
I fought with beasts, and three times saw
My children suffer by his law;
At last my own release was earned:
I was some time in being burned,
But at the close a Hand came through
The fire above my head, and drew
My soul to Christ, whom now I see.
Sergius, a brother, writes for me
This testimony on the wall—
For me, I have forgot it all.'
You say right; this were not so hard!
And since one nowise is debarred
From this, why not escape some sins
By such a method?"

X

Then begins
To the old point revulsion new—
(For 't is just this I bring you to)—
If after all we should mistake,
And so renounce life for the sake
Of death and nothing else? You hear
Each friend we jeered at, send the jeer
Back to ourselves with good effect—
"There were my beetles to collect!
My box—a trifle, I confess,
But here I hold it, ne'ertheless!"
Poor idiots, (let us pluck up heart
And answer) we, the better part

Have chosen, though 't were only hope,—
Nor envy moles like you that grope
Amid your veritable muck,
More than the grasshoppers would truck,
For yours, their passionate life away,
That spends itself in leaps all day
To reach the sun, you want the eyes
To see, as they the wings to rise
And match the noble hearts of them!
Thus the contemner we contemn,—
And, when doubt strikes us, thus we ward
Its stroke off, caught upon our guard,
—Not struck enough to overturn
Our faith, but shake it—make us learn
What I began with, and, I wis,
End, having proved,—how hard it is
To be a Christian!

XI

"Proved, or not,
Howe'er you wis, small thanks, I wot,
You get of mine, for taking pains
To make it hard to me. Who gains
By that, I wonder? Here I live
In trusting ease; and here you drive
At causing me to lose what most
Yourself would mourn for had you lost!"

XII

But, do you see, my friend, that thus
You leave Saint Paul for Æschylus?
—Who made his Titan's arch-device
The giving men blind hopes to spice
The meal of life with, else devoured
In bitter haste, while lo, death loured
Before them at the platter's edge!
If faith should be, as I allege,
Quite other than a condiment
To heighten flavors with, or meant
(Like that brave curry of his Grace)
To take at need the victuals' place?
If, having dined, you would digest
Besides, and turning to your rest
Should find instead ...

Now, you shall see
And judge if a mere foppery
Pricks on my speaking! I resolve
To utter—yes, it shall devolve
On you to hear as solemn, strange
And dread a thing as in the range
Of facts,—or fancies, if God will—
E'er happened to our kind! I still
Stand in the cloud and, while it wraps
My face, ought not to speak perhaps;
Seeing that if I carry through
My purpose, if my words in you
Find a live actual listener,
My story, reason must aver
False after all—the happy chance!
While, if each human countenance
I meet in London day by day,
Be what I fear,—my warnings fray
No one, and no one they convert,
And no one helps me to assert
How hard it is to really be
A Christian, and in vacancy
I pour this story!

I commence
By trying to inform you, whence
It comes that every Easter-night
As now, I sit up, watch, till light,
Upon those chimney-stacks and roofs,
Give, through my window-pane, gray proofs
That Easter-Day is breaking slow.
On such a night, three years ago,
It chanced that I had cause to cross
The common, where the chapel was,
Our friend spoke of, the other day—
You 've not forgotten, I dare say.
I fell to musing of the time
So close, the blessed matin-prime
All hearts leap up at, in some guise—
One could not well do otherwise.
Insensibly my thoughts were bent

Toward the main point; I overwent
Much the same ground of reasoning
As you and I just now. One thing
Remained, however—one that tasked
My soul to answer; and I asked,
Fairly and frankly, what might be
That History, that Faith, to me
—Me there—not me in some domain
Built up and peopled by my brain,
Weighing its merits as one weighs
Mere theories for blame or praise,
—The kingcraft of the Lucumons,
Or Fourier's scheme, its pros and cons,—
But my faith there, or none at all.
"How were my case, now, did I fall
Dead here, this minute—should I lie
Faithful or faithless?" Note that I
Inclined thus ever!—little prone
For instance, when I lay alone
In childhood, to go calm to sleep
And leave a closet where might keep
His watch perdue some murderer
Waiting till twelve o'clock to stir,
As good authentic legends tell:
"He might: but how improbable!
How little likely to deserve
The pains and trial to the nerve
Of thrusting head into the dark!"—
Urged my old nurse, and bade me mark
Beside, that, should the dreadful scout
Really lie hid there, and leap out
At first turn of the rusty key,
Mine were small gain that she could see,
Killed not in bed but on the floor,
And losing one night's sleep the more.
I tell you, I would always burst
The door ope, know my fate at first.
This time, indeed, the closet penned
No such assassin: but a friend
Rather, peeped out to guard me, fit
For counsel, Common Sense, to wit,
Who said a good deal that might pass,—
Heartening, impartial too, it was,
Judge else: "For, soberly now,—who
Should be a Christian if not you?"
(Hear how he smoothed me down.) "One takes
A whole life, sees what course it makes
Mainly, and not by fits and starts—

In spite of stoppage which imparts
Fresh value to the general speed.
A life, with none, would fly indeed:
Your progressing is slower—right!
We deal with progress and not flight.
Through baffling senses passionate,
Fancies as restless,—with a freight
Of knowledge cumbersome enough
To sink your ship when waves grow rough,
Though meant for ballast in the hold,—
I find, 'mid dangers manifold,
The good bark answers to the helm
Where faith sits, easier to o'erwhelm
Than some stout peasant's heavenly guide,
Whose hard head could not, if it tried,
Conceive a doubt, nor understand
How senses hornier than his hand
Should 'tice the Christian off his guard.
More happy! But shall we award
Less honor to the hull which, dogged
By storms, a mere wreck, waterlogged,
Masts by the board, her bulwarks gone
And stanchions going, yet bears on,—
Than to mere lifeboats, built to save,
And triumph o'er the breaking wave?
Make perfect your good ship as these,
And what were her performances!"
I added—"Would the ship reach home!
I wish indeed 'God's kingdom come'—
The day when I shall see appear
His bidding, as my duty, clear
From doubt! And it shall dawn, that day,
Some future season; Easter may
Prove, not impossibly, the time—
Yes, that were striking—fates would chime
So aptly! Easter-morn, to bring
The Judgment!—deeper in the spring
Than now, however, when there 's snow
Capping the hills; for earth must show
All signs of meaning to pursue
Her tasks as she was wont to do
—The skylark, taken by surprise
As we ourselves, shall recognize
Sudden the end. For suddenly
It comes; the dreadfulness must be
In that; all warrants the belief—
'At night it cometh like a thief.'
I fancy why the trumpet blows;

—Plainly, to wake one. From repose
We shall start up, at last awake
From life, that insane dream we take
For waking now, because it seems.
And as, when now we wake from dreams,
We laugh, while we recall them, 'Fool,
To let the chance slip, linger cool
When such adventure offered! Just
A bridge to cross, a dwarf to thrust
Aside, a wicked mage to stab—
And, lo ye, I had kissed Queen Mab!'
So shall we marvel why we grudged
Our labor here, and idly judged
Of heaven, we might have gained, but lose!
Lose? Talk of loss, and I refuse
To plead at all! You speak no worse
Nor better than my ancient nurse
When she would tell me in my youth
I well deserved that shapes uncouth
Frighted and teased me in my sleep:
Why could I not in memory keep
Her precept for the evil's cure?
'Pinch your own arm, boy, and be sure
You 'll wake forthwith!'"

And as I said
This nonsense, throwing back my head
With light complacent laugh, I found
Suddenly all the midnight round
One fire. The dome of heaven had stood
As made up of a multitude
Of handbreadth cloudlets, one vast rack
Of ripples infinite and black,
From sky to sky. Sudden there went,
Like horror and astonishment,
A fierce vindictive scribble of red
Quick flame across, as if one said
(The angry scribe of Judgment) "There—
Burn it!" And straight I was aware
That the whole ribwork round, minute
Cloud touching cloud beyond compute,
Was tinted, each with its own spot
Of burning at the core, till clot
Jammed against clot, and spilt its fire
Over all heaven, which 'gan suspire

As fanned to measure equable,—
Just so great conflagrations kill
Night overhead, and rise and sink,
Reflected. Now the fire would shrink
And wither off the blasted face
Of heaven, and I distinct might trace
The sharp black ridgy outlines left
Unburned like network—then, each cleft
The fire had been sucked back into,
Regorged, and out it surging flew
Furiously, and night writhed inflamed,
Till, tolerating to be tamed
No longer, certain rays world-wide
Shot downwardly. On every side
Caught past escape, the earth was lit;
As if a dragon's nostril split
And all his famished ire o'erflowed;
Then, as he winced at his lord's goad,
Back he inhaled: whereat I found
The clouds into vast pillars bound,
Based on the corners of the earth,
Propping the skies at top: a dearth
Of fire i' the violet intervals,
Leaving exposed the utmost walls
Of time, about to tumble in
And end the world.

XVI

I felt begin
The Judgment-Day: to retrocede
Was too late now. "In very deed,"
(I uttered to myself) "that Day!"
The intuition burned away
All darkness from my spirit too:
There, stood I, found and fixed, I knew,
Choosing the world. The choice was made;
And naked and disguiseless stayed,
And unevadable, the fact.
My brain held all the same compact
Its senses, nor my heart declined
Its office; rather, both combined
To help me in this juncture. I
Lost not a second,—agony
Gave boldness: since my life had end
And my choice with it—best defend,
Applaud both! I resolved to say,

"So was I framed by thee, such way
I put to use thy senses here!
It was so beautiful, so near,
Thy world,—what could I then but choose
My part there? Nor did I refuse
To look above the transient boon
Of time; but it was hard so soon
As in a short life, to give up
Such beauty: I could put the cup,
Undrained of half its fulness, by;
But, to renounce it utterly,
—That was too hard! Nor did the cry
Which bade renounce it, touch my brain
Authentically deep and plain
Enough to make my lips let go.
But thou, who knowest all, dost know
Whether I was not, life's brief while,
Endeavoring to reconcile
Those lips (too tardily, alas!)
To letting the dear remnant pass,
One day,—some drops of earthly good
Untasted! Is it for this mood,
That thou, whose earth delights so well,
Hast made its complement a hell?"

XVII

A final belch of fire like blood,
Overbroke all heaven in one flood
Of doom. Then fire was sky, and sky
Fire, and both, one brief ecstasy,
Then ashes. But I heard no noise
(Whatever was) because a voice
Beside me spoke thus, "Life is done,
Time ends, Eternity 's begun,
And thou art judged forevermore."

XVIII

I looked up; all seemed as before;
Of that cloud-Tophet overhead
No trace was left: I saw instead
The common round me, and the sky
Above, stretched drear and emptily
Of life. 'T was the last watch of night,
Except what brings the morning quite;

When the armed angel, conscience-clear,
His task nigh done, leans o'er his spear
And gazes on the earth he guards,
Safe one night more through all its wards,
Till God relieve him at his post.
"A dream—a waking dream at most!"
(I spoke out quick, that I might shake
The horrid nightmare off, and wake.)
"The world gone, yet the world is here?
Are not all things as they appear?
Is Judgment past for me alone?
—And where had place the great white throne?
The rising of the quick and dead?
Where stood they, small and great? Who read
The sentence from the opened book?"
So, by degrees, the blood forsook
My heart, and let it beat afresh;
I knew I should break through the mesh
Of horror, and breathe presently:
When, lo, again, the voice by me!

XIX

I saw ... O brother, 'mid far sands
The palm-tree-cinctured city stands,
Bright-white beneath, as heaven, bright-blue,
Leans o'er it, while the years pursue
Their course, unable to abate
Its paradisal laugh at fate!
One morn,—the Arab staggers blind
O'er a new tract of death, calcined
To ashes, silence, nothingness,—
And strives, with dizzy wits, to guess
Whence fell the blow. What if, 'twixt skies
And prostrate earth, he should surprise
The imaged vapor, head to foot,
Surveying, motionless and mute,
Its work, ere, in a whirlwind rapt
It vanish up again?—So hapt
My chance. He stood there. Like the smoke
Pillared o'er Sodom, when day broke,—
I saw him. One magnific pall
Mantled in massive fold and fall
His head, and coiled in snaky swathes
About his feet: night's black, that bathes
All else, broke, grizzled with despair,
Against the soul of blackness there.

A gesture told the mood within—
That wrapped right hand which based the chin,
That intense meditation fixed
On his procedure,—pity mixed
With the fulfilment of decree.
Motionless, thus, he spoke to me,
Who fell before his feet, a mass,
No man now.

XX

"All is come to pass.
Such shows are over for each soul
They had respect to. In the roll
Of Judgment which convinced mankind
Of sin, stood many, bold and blind,
Terror must burn the truth into:
Their fate for them!—thou hadst to do
With absolute omnipotence,
Able its judgments to dispense
To the whole race, as every one
Were its sole object. Judgment done,
God is, thou art,—the rest is hurled
To nothingness for thee. This world,
This finite life, thou hast preferred,
In disbelief of God's plain word,
To heaven and to infinity.
Here the probation was for thee,
To show thy soul the earthly mixed
With heavenly, it must choose betwixt.
The earthly joys lay palpable,—
A taint, in each, distinct as well;
The heavenly flitted, faint and rare,
Above them, but as truly were
Taintless, so, in their nature, best.
Thy choice was earth: thou didst attest
'T was fitter spirit should subserve
The flesh, than flesh refine to nerve
Beneath the spirit's play. Advance
No claim to their inheritance
Who chose the spirit's fugitive
Brief gleams, and yearned, 'This were to live
Indeed, if rays, completely pure
From flesh that dulls them, could endure,—
Not shoot in meteor-light athwart
Our earth, to show how cold and swart
It lies beneath their fire, but stand

As stars do, destined to expand,
Prove veritable worlds, our home!'
Thou saidst,—'Let spirit star the dome
Of sky, that flesh may miss no peak,
No nook of earth,—I shall not seek
Its service further!' Thou art shut
Out of the heaven of spirit; glut
Thy sense upon the world: 't is thine
Forever—take it!"

XXI

"How? Is mine,
The world?" (I cried, while my soul broke
Out in a transport.) "Hast thou spoke
Plainly in that? Earth's exquisite
Treasures of wonder and delight
For me?"

XXII

The austere voice returned,—
"So soon made happy? Hadst thou learned
What God accounteth happiness,
Thou wouldst not find it hard to guess
What hell may be his punishment
For those who doubt if God invent
Better than they. Let such men rest
Content with what they judged the best.
Let the unjust usurp at will:
The filthy shall be filthy still:
Miser, there waits the gold for thee!
Hater, indulge thine enmity!
And thou, whose heaven self-ordained
Was, to enjoy earth unrestrained,
Do it! Take all the ancient show!
The woods shall wave, the rivers flow,
And men apparently pursue
Their works, as they were wont to do,
While living in probation yet.
I promise not thou shalt forget
The past, now gone to its account;
But leave thee with the old amount
Of faculties, nor less nor more,
Unvisited, as heretofore,
By God's free spirit, that makes an end.

So, once more, take thy world! Expend
Eternity upon its shows
Flung thee as freely as one rose
Out of a summer's opulence,
Over the Eden-barrier whence
Thou art excluded. Knock in vain!"

XXIII

I sat up. All was still again.
I breathed free: to my heart, back fled
The warmth. "But, all the world!"—I said.
I stooped and picked a leaf of fern,
And recollected I might learn
From books, how many myriad sorts
Of fern exist, to trust reports,
Each as distinct and beautiful
As this, the very first I cull.
Think, from the first leaf to the last!
Conceive, then, earth's resources! Vast
Exhaustless beauty, endless change
Of wonder! And this foot shall range
Alps, Andes,—and this eye devour
The bee-bird and the aloe-flower?

XXIV

Then the voice: "Welcome so to rate
The arras-folds that variegate
The earth, God's antechamber, well!
The wise, who waited there, could tell
By these, what royalties in store
Lay one step past the entrance-door.
For whom, was reckoned, not too much,
This life's munificence? For such
As thou,—a race, whereof scarce one
Was able, in a million,
To feel that any marvel lay
In objects round his feet all day;
Scarce one, in many millions more,
Willing, if able, to explore
The secreter, minuter charm!
—Brave souls, a fern-leaf could disarm
Of power to cope with God's intent,—
Or scared if the south firmament
With north-fire did its wings refledge!

All partial beauty was a pledge
Of beauty in its plenitude:
But since the pledge sufficed thy mood,
Retain it! plenitude be theirs
Who looked above!"

XXV

Though sharp despairs
Shot through me, I held up, bore on.
"What matter though my trust were gone
From natural things? Henceforth my part
Be less with nature than with art!
For art supplants, gives mainly worth
To nature; 'tis man stamps the earth—
And I will seek his impress, seek
The statuary of the Greek,
Italy's painting—there my choice
Shall fix!"

XXVI

"Obtain it!" said the voice,
"The one form with its single act,
Which sculptors labored to abstract,
The one face, painters tried to draw,
With its one look, from throngs they saw.
And that perfection in their soul,
These only hinted at? The whole,
They were but parts of? What each laid
His claim to glory on?—afraid
His fellow-men should give him rank
By mere tentatives which he shrank
Smitten at heart from, all the more,
That gazers pressed in to adore!
'Shall I be judged by only these?'
If such his soul's capacities,
Even while he trod the earth,—think, now.
What pomp in Buonarroti's brow,
With its new palace-brain where dwells
Superb the soul, unvexed by cells
That crumbled with the transient clay!
What visions will his right hand's sway
Still turn to forms, as still they burst
Upon him? How will he quench thirst,
Titanically infantine,

Laid at the breast of the Divine?
Does it confound thee,—this first page
Emblazoning man's heritage?—
Can this alone absorb thy sight,
As pages were not infinite,—
Like the omnipotence which tasks
Itself to furnish all that asks
The soul it means to satiate?
What was the world, the starry state
Of the broad skies,—what, all displays
Of power and beauty intermixed,
Which now thy soul is chained betwixt,—
What else than needful furniture
For life's first stage? God's work, be sure.
No more spreads wasted, than falls scant!
He filled, did not exceed, man's want
Of beauty in this life. But through
Life pierce,—and what has earth to do,
Its utmost beauty's appanage,
With the requirement of next stage?
Did God pronounce earth 'very good'?
Needs must it he, while understood
For man's preparatory state;
Naught here to heighten nor abate;
Transfer the same completeness here,
To serve a new state's use,—and drear
Deficiency gapes every side!
The good, tried once, were bad, retried.
See the enwrapping rocky niche,
Sufficient for the sleep in which
The lizard breathes for ages safe:
Split the mould—and as light would chafe
The creature's new world-widened sense,
Dazzled to death at evidence
Of all the sounds and sights that broke
Innumerous at the chisel's stroke,—
So, in God's eye, the earth's first stuff
Was, neither more nor less, enough
To house man's soul, man's need fulfil.
Man reckoned it immeasurable?
So thinks the lizard of his vault!
Could God be taken in default,
Short of contrivances, by you,—
Or reached, ere ready to pursue
His progress through eternity?
That chambered rock, the lizard's world,
Your easy mallet's blow has hurled
To nothingness forever; so,

Has God abolished at a blow
This world, wherein his saints were pent,—
Who, though found grateful and content,
With the provision there, as thou,
Yet knew he would not disallow
Their spirit's hunger, felt as well,—
Unsated,—not unsatable,
As paradise gives proof. Deride
Their choice now, thou who sit'st outside!"

I cried in anguish: "Mind, the mind,
So miserably cast behind,
To gain what had been wisely lost!
Oh, let me strive to make the most
Of the poor stinted soul, I nipped
Of budding wings, else now equipped
For voyage from summer isle to isle!
And though she needs must reconcile
Ambition to the life on ground,
Still, I can profit by late found
But precious knowledge. Mind is best—
I will seize mind, forego the rest,
And try how far my tethered strength
May crawl in this poor breadth and length.
Let me, since I can fly no more,
At least spin dervish-like about
(Till giddy rapture almost doubt
I fly) through circling sciences,
Philosophies and histories!
Should the whirl slacken there, then verse,
Fining to music, shall asperse
Fresh and fresh fire-dew, till I strain
Intoxicate, half-break my chain!
Not joyless, though more favored feet
Stand calm, where I want wings to beat
The floor. At least earth's bond is broke!"

Then (sickening even while I spoke):
"Let me alone! No answer, pray,
To this! I know what thou wilt say!
All still is earth's,—to know, as much
As feel its truths, which if we touch

With sense, or apprehend in soul,
What matter? I have reached the goal—
'Whereto does knowledge serve!' will burn
My eyes, too sure, at every turn!
I cannot look back now, nor stake
Bliss on the race, for running's sake.
The goal's a ruin like the rest!"
"And so much worse thy latter quest,"
(Added the voice,) "that even on earth—
Whenever, in man's soul, had birth
Those intuitions, grasps of guess,
Which pull the more into the less,
Making the finite comprehend
Infinity,—the bard would spend
Such praise alone, upon his craft,
As, when wind-lyres obey the waft,
Goes to the craftsman who arranged
The seven strings, changed them and rechanged—
Knowing it was the South that harped.
He felt his song; in singing, warped;
Distinguished his and God's part: whence
A world of spirit as of sense
Was plain to him, yet not too plain,
Which he could traverse, not remain
A guest in:—else were permanent
Heaven on the earth its gleams were meant
To sting with hunger for full light,—
Made visible in verse, despite
The veiling weakness,—truth by means
Of fable, showing while it screens,—
Since highest truth, man e'er supplied,
Was ever fable on outside.
Such gleams made bright the earth an age;
Now the whole sun's his heritage!
Take up thy world, it is allowed,
Thou who hast entered in the cloud!"

XXIX

Then I—"Behold, my spirit bleeds,
Catches no more at broken reeds,—
But lilies flower those reeds above:
I let the world go, and take love!
Love survives in me, albeit those
I love be henceforth masks and shows,
Not living men and women: still
I mind how love repaired all ill,

Cured wrong, soothed grief, made earth amends
With parents, brothers, children, friends!
Some semblance of a woman yet
With eyes to help me to forget,
Shall look on me; and I will match
Departed love with love, attach
Old memories to new dreams, nor scorn
The poorest of the grains of corn
I save from shipwreck on this isle,
Trusting its barrenness may smile
With happy foodful green one day,
More precious for the pains. I pray,—
Leave to love, only!"

XXX

At the word,
The form, I looked to have been stirred
With pity and approval, rose
O'er me, as when the headsman throws
Axe over shoulder to make end—
I fell prone, letting him expend
His wrath, while thus the inflicting voice
Smote me. "Is this thy final choice?
Love is the best? 'Tis somewhat late!
And all thou dost enumerate
Of power and beauty in the world,
The mightiness of love was curled
Inextricably round about.
Love lay within it and without,
To clasp thee,—but in vain! Thy soul
Still shrunk from him who made the whole,
Still set deliberate aside
His love!—Now take love! Well betide
Thy tardy conscience! Haste to take
The show of love for the name's sake,
Remembering every moment who,
Beside creating thee unto
These ends, and these for thee, was said
To undergo death in thy stead
In flesh like thine: so ran the tale.
What doubt in thee could countervail
Belief in it? Upon the ground
'That in the story had been found
Too much love! How could God love so?'
He who in all his works below
Adapted to the needs of man,

Made love the basis of the plan,—
Did love, as was demonstrated:
While man, who was so fit instead
To hate, as every day gave proof,—Man
thought man, for his kind's behoof,
Both, could and did invent that scheme
Of perfect love: 'twould well beseem
Cain's nature thou wast wont to praise,
Not tally with God's usual ways!"

XXXI

And I cowered deprecatingly—
"Thou Love of God! Or let me die,
Or grant what shall seem heaven almost!
Let me not know that all is lost,
Though lost it be—leave me not tied
To this despair, this corpse-like bride!
Let that old life seem mine—no more—
With limitation as before,
With darkness, hunger, toil, distress:
Be all the earth a wilderness!
Only let me go on, go on,
Still hoping ever and anon
To reach one eve the Better Land!"

XXXII

Then did the form expand, expand—
I knew him through the dread disguise
As the whole God within his eyes
Embraced me.

XXXIII

When I lived again,
The day was breaking,—the gray plain
I rose from, silvered thick with dew.
Was this a vision? False or true?
Since then, three varied years are spent,
And commonly my mind is bent
To think it was a dream—be sure
A mere dream and distemperature—
The last day's watching: then the night,—
The shock of that strange Northern Light

Set my head swimming, bred in me
A dream. And so I live, you see,
Go through the world, try, prove, reject,
Prefer, still struggling to effect
My warfare; happy that I can
Be crossed and thwarted as a man,
Not left in God's contempt apart,
With ghastly smooth life, dead at heart,
Tame in earth's paddock as her prize.
Thank God, she still each method tries
To catch me, who may yet escape,
She knows,—the fiend in angel's shape!
Thank God, no paradise stands barred
To entry, and I find it hard
To be a Christian, as I said!
Still every now and then my head
Raised glad, sinks mournful—all grows drear
Spite of the sunshine, while I fear
And think, "How dreadful to be grudged
No ease henceforth, as one that's judged,
Condemned to earth forever, shut
From heaven!"
But Easter-Day breaks! But
Christ rises! Mercy every way
Is infinite,—and who can say?

Robert Browning – A Short Biography

He is the equal of any Victorian Poet that could be mentioned. However, Browning continues to be in the shadow of Tennyson, Arnold, Hopkins, Morris and many others.

Robert Browning was born on May 7th, 1812 in Walworth in the parish of Camberwell, London. He was baptized on June 14th, 1812, at Lock's Fields Independent Chapel, York Street, Walworth.

Browning's early years were certainly very interesting. His mother was an excellent pianist and a very devout evangelical Christian. His father, who worked as a clerk at the Bank of England, was also an artist, scholar, antiquarian, and collector of books and pictures. Indeed, he amassed more than 6,000 volumes of rare books including works in Greek, Hebrew, Latin, French, Italian, and Spanish. For the young and curious Browning, it was a wonderful resource, added to which his father was a guiding force in his education.

Many accounts attest that Browning was already proficient at reading and writing by the age of five. He is said to have been a bright but anxious student and to have studied and learnt Latin, Greek, and French by the time he was fourteen. From fourteen to sixteen he was educated at home, tutored in music, drawing, dancing, and horsemanship. Certainly, language and the arts were two areas the young Browning both absorbed and pushed himself towards.

At the age of twelve he wrote a volume of Byronic verse he called Incondita, which his parents attempted to have published. The attempts were unsuccessful and, disappointed, Browning destroyed the work.

In 1825, a cousin gave Browning a collection of Percy Bysshe Shelley's poetry; Browning was so enamored with the poems that he asked for the rest of Shelley's works for his thirteenth birthday. In fact, Browning then went the extra mile, declaring himself to be both a vegetarian and an atheist in honour of his hero.

Intriguingly it seems that the rejection of his first volume didn't dim his appreciation of other poets, but it appears to have stopped him writing any poems between the ages of thirteen and twenty.

In 1828, Browning enrolled at the newly-opened University of London. He was uncomfortable with the experience and he soon left, anxious to read and absorb at his own pace.

His education which, overall is notably rambling and lacks a structure that many of his artistic contemporaries enjoyed, i.e. excellent public schooling and then a degree at Oxford or Cambridge, may present many of his critics with ammunition to criticize, but alternatively his hap-hazard education certainly contributed to many of the references that baffled both critics and his audience, but they tellingly show the breath and scale of what he could turn words too. What others would call obscure references were, to Browning, remarkably obvious.

Browning's early career was very promising. His long poem Pauline (of which only a fragment was ever finished and published) brought him to the attention of the Pre-Raphaelite master Dante Gabriel Rossetti and his difficult Paracelsus (published in 1835) was warmly admired by both Dickens and Wordsworth.

In the 1830s he met the actor William Macready and was encouraged to develop and turn his talents to the stage by writing verse drama. But these plays, including Strafford, which ran for five nights in 1837, and those contained within the Bells and Pomegranates series, were, for the most part, unsuccessful.

During this period Browning began to discover that his real talents lay in taking a single character and allowing that character to discover more about himself by revealing further personal aspects of himself in his speeches; the dramatic monologue. The techniques he developed through this—especially the use of diction, rhythm, and symbol—are regarded as his most important contribution to poetry. They would later influence such major poets of the 20th Century as Ezra Pound, T. S. Eliot, and Robert Frost.

By 1840, with the publication of Sordello, the tide turned somewhat. Many thought he was being deliberately obscure, opaque beyond measure and his poetry for the next decade or so was not eagerly acquired or talked about.

As Browning attempted to rehabilitate his career he began a relationship with Elizabeth Barrett in 1845. He had read her poems and, being totally charmed by their quality, was determined to meet her. The poetess was better known than the younger Browning but suffered from a debilitating illness and was also subject to the harsh behaviour of her over-bearing father. Nevertheless, the new couple were soon inseparable.

Her father, as he did with any of his children that married, disinherited her. Despite this she had some money from her own resources and sensing that the best outcome for both the relationship and her own health was to move abroad the couple did just that. After a private marriage at St Marylebone Parish Church, in September 1846, they journeyed to Europe to honeymoon in Paris.

Their new life now took them to Italy, first to Pisa and a little later to Florence. There they absorbed life and one another.

But in the short term the literary assault on Browning's work did not let up. He was now criticized by such patrician writers as Charles Kingsley for his abandonment of England for foreign lands. Browning could do little to answer these attacks except to compose with his pen and continue with his poetical journey.

The Browning's were well respected, and even famous. Elizabeth health began to improve, she grew stronger and in 1849, at the age of 43, between four miscarriages, she gave birth to a son, Robert Wiedeman Barrett Browning, whom they nicknamed "Penini" or "Pen",

Intriguingly despite his growing reputation and return to form as a poet he was more often than not known as 'Elizabeth Barrett's husband'.

Work flowed from his pen that was to ensure his reputation as one of England's leading poets. When his collection Men and Women was published in 1855 it contained some of his finest lines. It was dedicated to Elizabeth. Life had begun to smile handsome rewards upon the Brownings.

Victorian society was very much taken with all things spiritualist. It was not enough to have command of much of the globe through Empire, they wished to know and explore wherever they could. The spirit world beckoned their interest. Browning dissented from this view believing it was all a hoax and a fraud. Elizabeth, however, was inclined to believe and this caused several disagreements between the couple.

They attended a séance by Daniel Dunglas Home, in July 1855. (Home was a famous and clamored after Scottish physical medium with the reported ability to levitate and speak with the dead). It is said that during this séance a spirit face materialised. Home then claimed it was the face of Browning's son who had died in infancy. Browning seized the 'materialisation' which turned out to be Home's bare foot. Browning had never lost a son in infancy.

After the séance, Browning wrote an angry letter to The Times, in which he said: "the whole display of hands, spirit utterances etc., was a cheat and imposture."

The Browning's time in Italy were immensely rewarding years for both their personal and professional lives. Browning encouraged her to include Sonnets from the Portuguese in her published works, these beautiful poems are undoubtedly one of the highlights of English love poetry.

Elizabeth had become quite politicised during these years. Engrossed in Italian politics (which was continuing to slowly re-unify the country), she issued a small volume of political poems entitled Poems before Congress (1860) most of which were written to express her sympathy with the Italian cause after the earlier outbreak of The Second Italian Independence War in 1859. In England they caused uproar. Conservative magazines such as Blackwood's and the Saturday Review labelled her a fanatic. She dedicated the book to her husband.

But in 1861 tragedy struck.

The couple had spent the winter of 1860–61 in Rome when Elizabeth's health deteriorated again and they returned to Florence in early June. However, these turned out to be her final weeks. Only morphine would now still the pain. She died in Browning's arms on June 29th, 1861. Browning said that she died "smilingly, happily, and with a face like a girl's .... Her last word was .... ''Beautiful''.

Her burial took place in the nearby Protestant English Cemetery of Florence. The local people were deeply saddened, and shops closed their doors in grief and respect.

Browning and their son were obviously devastated. Unable to bear being in Florence without Elizabeth they soon returned to London to live at 19 Warwick Crescent, Maida Vale.

As he re-integrated himself back into the London literary scene he began to finally receive the proper praise, respect and reputation that his works deserved.

Browning went on to publish Dramatis Personæ (1864), and The Ring and the Book (1868–1869). The latter, based on an "old yellow book" which told of a seventeenth-century Italian murder trial, received wide and generous critical acclaim. Although by now he was in the twilight of a long and prolific career, that had achieved some notable ups and downs, he was respected and indeed renowned for his talents and works.

In 1878, he revisited Italy for the first time since Elizabeth's death. He would return there on several further occasions but never to Florence.

Such was the esteem he was held in that The Browning Society was founded in 1881. Although he had never obtained a degree (something that set him apart from many other Victorian poets) he was now awarded honorary degrees from Oxford University in 1882 and then the University of Edinburgh in 1884.

In 1887, Browning produced the major work of his later years, Parleyings with Certain People of Importance in Their Day. Browning now spoke with his own voice as he engaged in a series of dialogues with long-forgotten figures of literary, artistic, and philosophic history. Unfortunately, both the critics and public were completely baffled by this.

On April 7th, 1889 Browning attended a dinner party at the home of his friend, the artist Rudolf Lehmann. The highlight of which was a recording made on a wax cylinder on an Edison cylinder phonograph. On the recording, which still exists, Browning recites part of How They Brought the Good News from Ghent to Aix, and can even be heard apologising when he forgets the words.

The recording was first played in 1890 on the anniversary of his death, at a gathering of his admirers, it was said to be the first time anyone's voice 'had been heard from beyond the grave'.

His last work Asolando: Fancies and Facts (1889), returned to his brief and concise lyric verse that was so popular. It was published on the day of his death on December 12th, 1889, Robert Browning was at his son's home Ca' Rezzonico in Venice.

He was buried in Poets' Corner in Westminster Abbey; his grave lies immediately adjacent to that of Alfred Tennyson.

Among the many who have publicly acknowledged their literary debt to him are Henry James, Oscar Wilde, George Bernard Shaw, G. K. Chesterton, Ezra Pound, Jorge Luis Borges, and Vladimir Nabokov.

Robert Browning - A Concise Bibliography

Here follows a list of the plays and poetry volumes published during his lifetime. Poems of particular worth are noted from within those volumes.

Pauline: A Fragment of a Confession (1833)
Paracelsus (1835)
Strafford (play) (1837)
Sordello (1840)
Bells and Pomegranates No. I: Pippa Passes (play) (1841)
    The Year's at the Spring
Bells and Pomegranates No. II: King Victor and King Charles (play) (1842)
Bells and Pomegranates No. III: Dramatic Lyrics (1842)
    Porphyria's Lover
    Soliloquy of the Spanish Cloister
    My Last Duchess
    The Pied Piper of Hamelin
    Count Gismond
    Johannes Agricola in Meditation
Bells and Pomegranates No. IV: The Return of the Druses (play) (1843)
Bells and Pomegranates No. V: A Blot in the 'Scutcheon (play) (1843)
Bells and Pomegranates No. VI: Colombe's Birthday (play) (1844)
Bells and Pomegranates No. VII: Dramatic Romances and Lyrics (1845)
    The Laboratory
    How They Brought the Good News from Ghent to Aix
    The Bishop Orders His Tomb at Saint Praxed's Church
    The Lost Leader
    Home Thoughts from Abroad
    Meeting at Night
Bells and Pomegranates No. VIII: Luria and A Soul's Tragedy (plays) (1846)
Christmas-Eve and Easter-Day (1850)
An Essay on Percy Bysshe Shelley (essay) (1852)
Two Poems (1854)
Men and Women (1855)
    Love Among the Ruins
    A Toccata of Galuppi's
    Childe Roland to the Dark Tower Came
    Fra Lippo Lippi
    Andrea Del Sarto
    The Patriot

www.ingramcontent.com/pod-product-compliance
Lightning Source LLC
Chambersburg PA
CBHW070113070426
42448CB00038B/2643